WINNING SPIRITUAL BATTLES

WINNING SPIRITUAL BATTLES
A Practical Guide To Help You Win

BLAKE J. MELANCON

XULON PRESS

Xulon Press
2301 Lucien Way #415
Maitland, FL 32751
407.339.4217
www.xulonpress.com

© 2023 by Blake J. Melancon

All rights reserved solely by the author. The author guarantees all contents are original and do not infringe upon the legal rights of any other person or work. No part of this book may be reproduced in any form without the permission of the author.

Due to the changing nature of the Internet, if there are any web addresses, links, or URLs included in this manuscript, these may have been altered and may no longer be accessible. The views and opinions shared in this book belong solely to the author and do not necessarily reflect those of the publisher. The publisher therefore disclaims responsibility for the views or opinions expressed within the work.

Unless otherwise indicated, Scripture quotations taken from the New King James Version (NKJV). Copyright © 1982 by Thomas Nelson, Inc. Used by permission. All rights reserved.

Paperback ISBN-13: 978-1-66288-123-7

Ebook ISBN-13: 978-1-66288-124-4

Contents

Chapter 1	Identity Crisis	1
Chapter 2	Taking Your Thoughts Captive	17
Chapter 3	Unconfessed Sin	25
Chapter 4	Spiritual Neutrality	29
Chapter 5	Be Available	43
Chapter 6	I Am Not My Own	61
Chapter 7	Firstfruits	69

Foreword

Since the main purpose of a book's foreword is to promote the work by establishing the author's credibility, this will be an extremely easy task! Reverend Blake Melancon is a man who everyone should want in their corner! I first met Blake and his lovely wife, Cristina, when they joined Exciting Immanuel in El Paso, Texas which I had the privilege of pastoring for 16 wonderful years. The first thing I learned about Blake is that his last name is Cajun and is not pronounced like it looks, but rather, "Meh-lawn'-sown"! When Blake steps into a room, the place lights up! He has an infectious and magnetic personality which enabled him to be very successful in the business world and as a believer in Jesus Christ. When you read this book you will immediately feel his love for the Lord and grasp his enthusiasm for teaching God's truth!

Blake is a natural leader and was an outstanding example to our men, soon becoming a powerful voice for Christian men's ministry in El Paso. He is affectionately called "Coach Blake" by many of his friends because he has spent years as a volunteer and High School coach for boys' athletics. He founded "G.A.M.E" (God's Army of Men Excelling) and not only led a city-wide men's gathering in one of El Paso's largest outdoor arenas, but also had his own weekly Men's radio talk show, "In The Game with Coach Blake." One of the reasons Blake makes such a strong connection with men is this love for sports and he successfully uses many sports analogies in his teaching (Beware: He is a die-hard LSU Tigers fan!)

In addition to being a great teacher and mentor, Blake is a sought after motivational speaker who loves to "fire up" people for Jesus! He has never known a stranger and has a heart of compassion when it comes to helping and counseling people who find themselves down and out.

Winning Spiritual Battles will give you clear steps in how to walk in victory and experience supernatural living! Blake has come from a background of being abused as a child to walking the victorious Christian life as a strong husband, father, pastor, and community leader. You will learn through his strong testimony that God never wastes a hurt and that you are a mighty work of God in progress! This book will help you move from feeling like a victim to being a victor, because as the author says, **"You cannot have power in the present and future while holding onto the past."**

If you struggle with your thought life, you will learn how to take those unspiritual thoughts captive by establishing a spiritual "first alert" system in your mind, driving out negative thoughts and replacing them with spiritual elements that will keep you on the safe path of righteousness. If you want to really be a winner in life and leave a lasting spiritual legacy, then *Winning*

Foreword

Spiritual Battles is a must-read and a book you need to teach to your children!

Rix W. Tillman, D.Min
Retired Pastor, Author, Speaker
Past President, SBOT Pastors' Conference

Winning Spiritual Battles is not your run of the mill intellectual, theoretical journey into the realm of spiritual disciplines. Rather it is an open and honest description of one man's experience in following after God. Blake Melancon does not sugar coat the Christian life he has lived. His open vulnerability in sharing how his youthful innocence was affected by the depravity of humanity is heartbreaking. But his declaration of God's goodness and power in delivering him and using him is inspiring. Come along as Blake puts everyday work clothes on scripture and walks it through real life situations demonstrating how you can win life's spiritual battles through God's power.

Jim Mullen, Pastor, Former International Director of Training (BGEA) Billy Graham Evangelistic Association

Introduction

I knew it was going to be another night of torment, another sleepless night of feeling alone, helpless, and abandoned as his advances kept coming. Why doesn't anyone help me? Where has everyone gone? The darkness pierced the night, and the abuse pierced my soul.

I know now that the enemy had declared war on me, and at the age of ten I followed him into twenty years of a lifestyle of drugs, alcohol, sex, and sin. At the age of ten, I was repeatedly sexually abused by a member of my family. This happened in my own home, in my own bed. When I was twelve years old, I was again sexually abused in a public restroom by a stranger. I was also verbally, physically, and mentally abused by my father. I began using drugs when I was ten, and for the next twenty years of my life, I used hate, anger, bitterness, violence, drugs, alcohol, sex, and any other thing I could do to ease the pain of the abuse.

When someone is sexually abused, he or she stops growing emotionally. It is not until one deals with the abuse, forgives, and starts the healing process that the emotional state of the abused person starts to become stable again. The Holy Spirit takes us through a process that heals us physically, mentally, emotionally, and spiritually.

My wife, Cristina, and I married when I was twenty-eight years old. She was dealing with a grown man with the emotions of a ten-year-old. I felt like my life was lost, and I had been losing for nearly twenty years until the day I met Jesus Christ, my Lord and Savior. On that day, God miraculously reached down and delivered me. For the first time in my life, I felt loved and cared for, and I was no longer alone. God delivered me from a thousand-dollar-a-week cocaine habit and a life of sex, drugs, and rock-n-roll. This was February 26, 1990. I thank God for Linda Burgos for leading me to Christ. My life has never been the same.

After a few years as a follower of Christ, I knew there was something missing. I still fought the battles of my past, and I was losing a lot of them. It was not until I became desperate and got down on my knees that I was delivered. I cried out to God to take away anything that was hindering my relationship with Him, and He answered my cry for help.

I began to remember the abuse that I had buried so deep, and the Holy Spirit was telling me I had to forgive all the abusers in my past. The journey to healing began when I forgave my abusers. All the hatred I had for everyone is now being replaced with the love of Jesus Christ. The healing process continues today.

It is a refining process in my spirit, just like the refining of silver mentioned in the Bible: *"Take away the dross from silver, And it will go to the silversmith for jewelry"* (Prov. 25:4)

Introduction

Dross represents the impurities we have in our lives that must rise to the top and be scooped out to refine us into the people He wants us to be. Silver must be crushed and heated to over 800°C to remove all the impurities to make jewelry. God often must take us through the furnaces of life (trials and tribulations) to refine us. God did it to His chosen people:

> *Behold, I have refined you, but not as silver; I have tested you in the furnace of affliction.* (Isa. 48:10).

> *I will bring the one-third through the fire, Will refine them as silver is refined, and test them as gold is tested. They will call on My name, And I will answer them. I will say, "This is My people"; And each one will say, "The LORD is my God."* (Zech. 13:9).

Coming from a very abusive background and losing my childhood innocence at an early age, I have fought these battles. Through the grace, mercy, love, and power of the blood of Jesus and the Holy Spirit, I have won many battles and have been delivered from much bondage in my life. I have experienced the practical steps I suggest in this book. I know they work because not only have I used them to have victory and have also helped others achieve victory and be set free from their abusive pasts.

This is a lifelong journey, but with the help of Christian trauma counselors and being empowered by The Holy Spirit, I win more battles than I lose.

It doesn't matter how much you have been hurt; God knows. God wants to set you free today and help you win! I want to help you win the spiritual battles in your life. I want to share something with you that God revealed to me many years ago:

God never wastes a hurt!

You see, with Christ guiding our lives and living inside of us, we have the power of the Holy Spirit to overcome and have victory in our lives. God wants to give us a new start today! God's Word says, *"Therefore, if anyone is in Christ, he is a new creation; old things have passed away; behold, all things have become new"* (2 Cor. 5:17).

Sometimes for God to use us, we must go through the furnace of affliction to be purified before Him.

It's not what happens to us in life, it's what we do about it.

The world tells us that we need to look a certain way, dress a certain way, drink the right drinks, and drive the right cars. We are bombarded with ads on TV, social media, radio and magazines, proclaiming: "You need more of [fill in the blank] to be somebody." Everyone is trying to "keep up with the Joneses."

In doing so, we take on someone else's identity. Our children want to be superheroes, and our teenagers want to dress and look like the latest star or teen idol. The mantra popular with the younger generation is, "YOLO"—you only live once—so we need to grab everything we can to be somebody in the world. The Bible gives us a different message. We can't win the battles and walk in victory, playing by the world's rules. However, God wants us to win the spiritual battles by implementing His game plan. Maybe you have been told your whole life, "You're never going to amount to anything!" You think you'll never make it. You might have feelings of guilt, bitterness, or unworthiness. You feel like nothing you ever do is good enough. Guilt is one of Satan's chief weapons against you. Bitterness is another one of the enemy's weapons. If Satan can keep you believing his lies, he will win many battles against you.

- If you must have the approval of others, you are losing the battle.

- If you must have recognition in everything you do, you are losing the battle.

Little babies cry for it, old men die for it—recognition!

You feel like you must have an important title or an important job to be someone. You can't walk in the supernatural power of God feeling shameful, guilty, unworthy, and insufficient. God wants you to walk in victory! God wants you to walk in power! God wants you to live in His supernatural Spirit and win the battles you are fighting.

I began a supernatural journey God had planned for me all along. I knew for the first time, I could win! I realized that what the enemy Satan tried to destroy through abuse, God would use to equip me for His work. I want to share what God has revealed to me and hope and pray it will help you win the spiritual battles that you face so you can walk in victory. You cannot understand the supernatural mind and things of God while living in the natural. God supernaturally gives you understanding through His Word and the Holy Spirit. The following Bible verse is very important to understanding what God says about the natural man: *"But the natural man does not receive the things of the Spirit of God, for they are foolishness to him; nor can he know them, because they are spiritually discerned"* (1 Cor. 2:14).

To walk in victory and experience supernatural living, we must be spiritually discerning. We must have the mind of Christ. How do we receive the mind of Christ? By accepting God's Son, Jesus Christ, who died on the cross for our sins. Jesus specifically told Nicodemus how to spend eternity with God. In John, chapter 3, Jesus explains to Nicodemus, how to be born again:

> *[1] There was a man of the Pharisees named Nicodemus, a ruler of the Jews. [2] This man came to Jesus by night and said to Him, "Rabbi, we know that You are a teacher come from God; for no one can do these signs that You do unless God is with him." [3] Jesus answered and said to him, "Most assuredly, I say to you, unless one is born again, he cannot see the kingdom of God." [4] Nicodemus said to Him, "How can a man be born when he is old? Can he enter a second time into his mother's womb and be born?" [5] Jesus answered, "Most assuredly, I say to you, unless one is born of water and the Spirit, he cannot enter the kingdom of*

God. *⁶ That which is born of the flesh is flesh, and that which is born of the Spirit is spirit. ⁷ Do not marvel that I said to you, "You must be born again."* (John 3:1–7)

The one and only way to heaven is through Jesus Christ. You might be reading this right now and asking, "What do I need to be saved from?" This is a great question. Although we may have lived a morally good life, never stolen money, never murdered anyone, and have always been a good person, we can never be *good enough* to get to heaven. The Word of God tells us no one is righteous: *"As it is written: "There is none righteous, no, not one" (Rom. 3:10),* and *"For all have sinned and fall short of the glory of God" (Rom. 3:23).*

Religion will not get us into heaven! We might think that going to church will get us into heaven. I have heard it said, "Those people have been in church their entire lives. They have positions in the church. They know all the terminology, and they sound very religious." Do you know people like this? There is only one way into heaven, and it is not by or through religion! The Bible clearly states that none of us will get into heaven because we:

* Do the best we can

* Believe in God

* Try to keep the Ten Commandments

* Never hurt anyone

* Are members of a church

* Are baptized

* Receive any sacraments from the church

* Do any human effort, typically referred to as "works."

Works will not get us into heaven! If we could work our way to heaven, we would not need a Savior. Getting to heaven would totally depend on the things we do. Our efforts, no matter how much or how good they are, they are not good enough. It's only by God's grace we are saved: "*[8]For by grace are you saved through faith, and that not of yourselves; it is the gift of God, [9] not of works, lest anyone should boast*" *(Eph. 2:8–9)*. There's nothing we can do to get into heaven. Christ has already paid the price. We must be willing to accept His sacrifice for our eternal reward.

Here's the great news: God loves us, and He wants to spend eternity with us.

> *For God so loved the world that He gave His only begotten Son, that whoever believes in Him should not perish but have everlasting life.* [17] *For God did not send His Son into the world to condemn the world, but that the world through Him might be saved. (John 3:16–17)*

> *But God demonstrates His own love toward us, in that while we were still sinners, Christ died for us. (Romans 5:8)*

Introduction

This is God's remedy for sin. It is a gift from God, but we must repent and receive the gift. Someone can buy a gift for us, wrap it up in beautiful paper, and put the most exquisite bow on it. They may hold it out for us to take it, but it is not ours until we receive it and possess it. God has the gift and is offering it to us, but we must receive the precious gift of eternal life.

> *For the wages of sin is death, but the gift of God is eternal life in Christ Jesus our Lord. (Rom. 6:23)*

> *But as many as received Him, to them He gave the right to become children of God, to those who believe in His name. (John 1:12)*

God wants us to be saved. God created us to have fellowship with Him. His desire is to spend eternity with us. For *"whoever calls on the name of the LORD ... shall be saved"* (Rom. 10:13)

Here are the keys to beginning a new life, winning, and walking in victory:

- Accepting Jesus's death for all of our sins.

- Believing that the Lord Jesus Christ died on the cross, was raised from the dead, and is dwelling with our Father in heaven.

- Confessing to God that we are sinners. Realizing that every sin we have ever committed is against Almighty God.

Here is what the Word of God says about how to accept Jesus Christ as our Lord and Savior. We must repent to receive God's marvelous gift of salvation:

> *that if you confess with your mouth the Lord Jesus and believe in your heart that God has raised Him from the dead, you will be saved. [10] For with the heart one believes unto righteousness, and with the mouth confession is made unto salvation. (Rom. 10:9–10)*

> *Most assuredly, I say to you, he who hears My word and believes in Him who sent Me has everlasting life, and shall not come into judgment, but has passed from death into life. [25] "Most assuredly, I say to you, the hour is coming, and now is, when the dead will hear the voice of the Son of God; and those who hear will live. (John 5:24–25)*

> *but these are written that you may believe that Jesus is the Christ, the Son of God, and that believing you may have life in His name. (John 20:31)*

This is not a "hope so," or a "maybe so." This is a "know so," that heaven will be our eternal home.

> *These things I have written to you who believe in the name of the Son of God, **that you may know that you have eternal life**, and that you may continue to believe in the name of the Son of God. (1 John 5:13)*

Introduction

Let this become the greatest day of our lives by receiving God's gift of eternal life. To do so, pray this prayer:

Dear Lord Jesus,

I know I am a sinner, and I need forgiveness from You, Lord Jesus. I repent of all my sins. I believe that You, Jesus, died on the cross and rose again so that I may have eternal life. I turn away from my sins and ask for forgiveness from You. Right now, I invite You into my heart to be my Savior and Lord. From this day forward, I am born again. Thank you for hearing my prayer and giving me Your gift of eternal life. In Jesus Christ's name, Amen.

I remember as I prayed that prayer that God was miraculously breaking the chains of addiction from around my neck. I am so grateful I prayed that prayer. My life was transformed for eternity.

Praise the Lord! If you just prayed that prayer, truly believed and repented, you are now a child of God. You were born a creation of God, but now you are a child of the King of kings and Lord of lords. You are ready for supernatural living. You are ready to *win today!* You should not think like you thought before. You should not walk like you walked before. You are ready for His fresh anointing of His supernatural Spirit. As you read the following pages, I pray that God uses these words to help you in your walk with Jesus Christ.

> **Win Point:**
> Who I am, and all I ever will be, hinges on God's grace in my life!

There are three steps of obedience that God wants you to take:

- Accept His Son Jesus Christ as your Savior,

- Be scripturally baptized, and

- Go tell others about the Good News of Jesus's saving power.

The other thing God wants you to do now that you're born again, is to find a good life-giving, Bible-believing church. Find a place where you can belong and start to grow in your walk with Christ. You have a new identity in Jesus! Go forward and *win* the spiritual battles!

> **Win Point:**
> We are not who we used to be!
> We are not who we want to be!
> We are not who we are going to be!
> We are a mighty work of God in progress!

CHAPTER 1
IDENTITY CRISIS

The Bible clearly states that you are somebody to God. You are worthy of the blessings your Lord and Savior wants to bestow upon you. You are important to the Creator of the universe. The world and even your own family might tell you otherwise, but your heavenly Father tells you something far different. The following scriptures were written to let us know we are somebody in God's eyes, and we can begin walking in our inheritance.

Many people sit and dream of having a rich family member who will leave an inheritance to them. God, our Father, has left the greatest inheritance for you. His Word says you are a co-heir with Christ. Wow—an inheritance that is everlasting! The foundation of a supernatural life as a born-again believer is knowing who you are in Christ. So many times, I have heard, "I am just a sinner saved by grace." That is great news, but we are much more than that. Don't just take my word for it, but let's take a thirty-one-day journey into God's exciting, living, identifying Word.

We are not defined:

- By our past.

- What people say.

- What the world expects.

Let the Word of God define who you are, not your past or other people.

The Bible tells us we are much more than just sinners saved by grace. We are somebody; we are born again into a royal blood line, and we are royalty! Let's look at who God says we are.

I want to give you thirty-one days of Bible verses and affirmations to help you know who you are in Christ.

Every day, use one of the corresponding Bible verses and affirmations to start your day.

THIRTY-ONE CONFESSIONS TO WIN SPIRITUAL BATTLES

1. I am salt of the earth.

> *You are the salt of the earth; but if the salt loses its flavor, how shall it be seasoned? It is then good for nothing but to be thrown out and trampled underfoot by men. (Matt. 5:13)*

Salt is used for seasoning and for preservation. We, through our walk as believers, are called by God to season the lost. We must add holy flavoring to a dying world. If we do not walk the walk of a believer, we will lose our flavor and will be of no use in the kingdom of God. Salt was and still is, in some circumstances, used for preserving things. We are called by our heavenly Father to preserve His heritage. Just as salt gives food life, we are to add life to others.

2. I am the light of the world.

> *You are the light of the world. A city that is set on a hill cannot be hidden. Let your light so shine before men, that they may see your good works and glorify your Father in heaven. (Matt. 5:14, 16)*

Darkness is a relative absence of visible light. The world is a dark place, and the light is growing dimmer. Our walk as a believer should shine with such a bright light that it will show the lost the way they should go. Our lifestyle should shine like a brilliant beacon in the world around us.

Every time we walk into a room, it should become illuminated. Our nickname should be "Sunshine" because we should brighten up a room when we walk into it. That's the walk God wants us to have.

3. I am a child of God.

> *But as many as received Him, to them He gave the right to become children of God, to those who believe in His name. (John 1:12)*

What a privilege it is to be called "a child of God." The Creator of the universe calls us His child. When we receive His Son, Jesus Christ, we become His child. Imagine a Father who knows our future, who even knows the number of hairs on our head. Our heavenly Father knows our future and is always present in the form of the Holy Spirit to help us.

4. I am part of the true vine.

> *I am the true vine, and My Father is the vinedresser. Every branch in Me that does not bear fruit He takes away; and every branch that bears fruit He prunes, that it may bear more fruit. You are already clean because of the word which I have spoken to you. Abide in Me, and I in you. As the branch cannot bear fruit of itself, unless it abides in the vine, neither can you, unless you abide in Me. I am the vine; you are the branches. He who abides in Me, and I in him, bears much fruit; for without Me you can do nothing. (John 15:1–5)*

We have all been part of a team, group, or organization. Now that we are children of God, we are a branch of the true Vine that has the greatest root system ever known. This Vine has the best fertilizer and soil to feed His branches. This is the work of the indwelling of the Holy Spirit. He wants our branches to tap into His greatness. When we tap into Him, we will grow and be strong. When we become strong, we can weather every storm and bear fruit.

5. I am Christ's friend.

No longer do I call you servants, for a servant does not know what his master is doing; but I have called you friends, for all things that I heard from My Father I have made known to you. (John 15:15)

We have never had a friend like Jesus. He will never leave us or fail us. He is with us all the time. When everyone else walks out, He is still there. When everyone else has let us down, He is there to pick us up. Imagine a friend that loves us unconditionally. What a friend we have in Jesus!

6. I am chosen and appointed by God to bear His fruit.

You did not choose Me, but I chose you and appointed you that you should go and bear fruit, and that your fruit should remain, that whatever you ask the Father in My name He may give you. (John 15:16)

We are appointed to bear fruit. How awesome is that? He chose us to bear fruit for His kingdom. That means we have all the tools necessary to bear fruit. All we must do is ask. If a fruit tree does not bear fruit, something is wrong. If a believer is not bearing fruit, something is wrong. Let's go *win today* and bear fruit!

7. I am a slave to righteousness.

And having been set free from sin, you became slaves of righteousness. (Rom. 6:18)

We are no longer slaves to sin but slaves to righteousness. We may sin, but now we have the ability to live above being a slave to sin. We can be free from habitual, continual sin. We have the ability through the Holy Spirit to live holy and righteous lives.

8. I am enslaved to God.

But now having been set free from sin, and having become slaves of God, you have your fruit to holiness, and the end, everlasting life. (Rom. 6:22)

The benefit of being enslaved to Christ is the sanctification process (when we confess our sins, God forgives us, cleans us up again, and set us apart to be life-giving).

Here is a great Bible verse that explains sanctification: *"If we confess our sins, He is faithful and just to forgive us our sins and to cleanse us from all unrighteousness" (1 John 1:9)*

We are justified at the point of accepting Jesus Christ as our Lord and Savior. Sanctification is an ongoing process that we, as believers, are constantly going through on earth.

9. I am joint heirs with Christ and heirs of God our Father.

And if children, then heirs—heirs of God and joint heirs with Christ, if indeed we suffer with Him, that we may also be glorified together. (Rom. 8:17)

The word *heir* is defined like this, "a person who inherits or has a right of inheritance in the property of another following the latter's death." Believers are heirs of God and co-heirs with Jesus to the eternal kingdom of God. In this context, it indicates that believers have been given the full privileges of being part of God's family.

10. I am a temple of God. His spirit dwells in me.

Do you not know that you are a temple of God and that Spirit of God dwells in you? . . . Or do you know that your body is a temple of the Holy Spirit who is in you, whom you have from God, and you are not your own? For you were bought at a price: therefore glorify God in your body and in your spirit, which are God's. (1 Cor. 3:16; 6:19–20)

We must keep the temple clean. As a believer, we are now the temple of God. This is an awesome responsibility. The old saying, "To whom much is given, much is expected," applies here. God has given us eternal life, so He expects us to live holy and righteous lives.

11. I am joined with the Lord and am one with Him.

But he who is joined to the Lord is one spirit with Him. (1 Cor. 6:17)

His Spirit and our spirit are joined. This is the mystery of the Holy Spirit living inside of us. My friend, this is the most amazing thing that happens in our lives. We are one spirit with God.

12. I am a member of Christ's body.

Now you are the body of Christ, and members individually. (1 Cor. 12:27)

Though we are all very different, we are still members of the body of Christ. We all have different gifts and functions within the body. All members of the body are important. We are part of the most important body, the body of Christ!

13. I am a new creation.

Therefore, if anyone is in Christ, he is a new creation; old things have passed away, behold, all things have become new. (2 Cor. 5:17)

Imagine all our sins gone. All the sins, from the time we were born until we accepted Jesus Christ as our Lord and Savior, are washed away. You were an alcoholic; now you are a new creation. You were a drug addict; now you are a new creation. You're not what you once were. You are new! Now we can start winning the spiritual battles that lie ahead.

14. I am a minister of reconciliation.

Now all things are of God, who has reconciled us to Himself through Jesus Christ, and has given us the ministry of reconciliation. (2 Cor. 5:18)

He has reconciled the broken relationship mankind has had since Adam and Eve! He has made it right through Jesus Christ. We are not transformed or reconciled until we accept His Son as Lord and Savior. We, in turn, should tell as many people as possible about the reconciliation of God through His Son. This is our commission.

15. I am an ambassador for Christ.

Now then, we are ambassadors for Christ, as though God were pleading through us: we implore you on Christ's behalf, be reconciled to God. (2 Cor. 5:20)

An ambassador is an individual selected to represent their country. He/she is the person that speaks on behalf of their country. An ambassador is the liaison for that country. We, as children of God, have been chosen to be His ambassadors. As an ambassador, we should be telling others about the wonderful kingdom of God we now represent.

16. I am a son of God.

For you are all sons of God through faith in Christ Jesus. (Gal. 3:26)

This is amazing! We are children of the Most High God. He allows us to be called a family member. We can call Him Father because He calls us His children.

17. I am one with Jesus Christ.

There is neither Jew nor Greek, there is neither slave nor free, there is neither male nor female; for you are all one in Christ Jesus. (Gal. 3:28)

When the Holy Spirit takes up residence in us, we become one with Him. Can you imagine Jesus loves us so much, that He makes us one with Him? We are one with the Messiah, one with our Lord and Savior.

18. I am an heir to God.

[6] And because you are sons, God has sent forth the Spirit of His Son into your hearts, crying out, "Abba, Father!" [7] Therefore you are no longer a slave but a son, and if a son, then an heir of God through Christ. (Gal. 4:6–7)

Most people are fascinated with royalty. Wouldn't you love to be an heir to royalty? Here's the good news: we are! We are heirs to the King of kings and Lord of lords. As heirs, our inheritance is eternal life with Almighty God.

19. I am a saint.

Paul, an apostle of Jesus Christ by the will of God, to the saints who are in Ephesus, and faithful in Christ Jesus. (Eph. 1:1)

We are more than just sinners saved by grace! We are saints! Once we have accepted Jesus Christ as our Lord and Savior, we become saints in God's eyes. This should help us understand just how much we truly mean to God.

20. I am God's workmanship, created in Christ to do His work.

For we are His workmanship, created in Christ Jesus for good works, which God prepared beforehand that we should walk in them. (Eph. 2:10)

God created us, and He has great plans for our lives. Before the foundation of the earth, God planned great things for us. What we must do is step into God's awesome plan for our lives.

21. I am a fellow citizen with the rest of the people in God's family.

> *Now, therefore, you are no longer strangers and foreigners, but fellow citizens with the saints and members of the household of God. (Eph. 2:19)*

His Word assures us that we have a place in the household of God. We are not strangers, but members of His household. We don't have to knock on the door; we have a key to the entire house. This is tremendous news! When Satan tries to make us feel like we are nothing, remember we are fellow citizens and members of the household of God.

22. I am righteous and holy.

> *And that you put on the new man which was created according to God, in true righteousness and holiness. (Eph. 4:24)*

This is not self-righteousness. We are made righteous and holy through the blood shed by Christ Jesus. We must put on the righteousness of God!

23. I am a citizen of heaven.

> *For our citizenship is in heaven, from which we also eagerly wait for the Savior, the Lord Jesus Christ. (Phil. 3:20)*

It is such a privilege to be a citizen of the United States. However, this is nothing compared to being a citizen of heaven with God for all eternity! We are just passing through this earth, but our ultimate citizenship is in heaven!

24. I am hidden with Christ in God.

For you died, and your life is hidden with Christ in God. (Col. 3:3)

Many spiritual things we know are hidden from the world. We now have access to the supernatural, spiritual world of God.

25. I am an expression of the life of Christ because He is my life.

When Christ who is our life appears, then you also will appear with Him in glory. (Col. 3:4)

This is incredible news! When Christ comes back, we will be with Him.

26. I am chosen by God, holy and dearly loved.

Therefore, as the elect of God, holy and beloved, put-on tender mercies, kindness, humility, meekness, longsuffering. (Col. 3:12)

God chose us! We are God's elect! We are holy and beloved! We must put on tender mercies, kindness, humility, meekness, and longsuffering.

27. I am a child of light and not of darkness.

You are all sons of light and sons of the day. We are not of the night nor of darkness. (1 Thess. 5:5)

When we become a child of God, we should become light in this dark world. Our life should be a shining example to others who don't know Jesus Christ as their Lord and Savior. Before our transformation by the Holy Spirit, we were children of darkness. Now, we are children of the light. Hallelujah!

28. I am a holy brother, a partaker of a heavenly calling.

Therefore, holy brethren, partakers of the heavenly calling, consider the Apostle and High Priest of our confession, Christ Jesus. (Heb. 3:1)

We are not holy on our own but are made holy through the blood of Jesus Christ. We should thank God every day for making us holy and allowing us to partake in His heavenly calling.

29. I am a partaker of Christ; I share in His life.

For we have become partakers of Christ if we hold the beginning of our confidence steadfast to the end. (Heb. 3:14)

God says we have become partakers, or a part, of Christ. We must hold on to the confidence we have in Jesus Christ. Our confidence cannot be in ourselves but always in who He is.

30. I am chosen by God to proclaim His excellencies.

But you are a chosen generation, a royal priesthood, a holy nation, His own special people, that you may proclaim the praises of Him who called you out of darkness into His marvelous light; who once were not a people but are now the people of God, who had not obtained mercy but now have obtained mercy. (1 Pet. 2:9–10)

Praise the Lord! We are chosen, we are royalty, we are holy, and we are here to proclaim all the excellent characteristics that God possesses. He called us out of darkness and into His light. He poured out His mercy so that we could be part of who He is.

31. I am now a child of God, and I resemble Christ.

Behold what manner of love the Father has bestowed on us, that we should be called children of God! Therefore, the world does not know us, because it did not know Him. Beloved, now we are children of God; and it has not yet been revealed what we shall be, but we know that when He is revealed, we shall be like Him, for we shall see Him as He is. (1 John 3:1–2)

Awesome, is all I can say every time I read in the Bible who I am in Christ. We are important to God. Take one of these scriptures each day and memorize it to start learning who you are in Christ.

Knowing who you are in Christ is the foundation for walking in victory and power.

The enemy will always whisper that you are nothing and not important to anyone. Why would God possibly make you an heir and a joint heir to His kingdom if you are not important to Him? Realize that the Bible is the Truth, and whatever the Bible says about you is true for today and the rest of your life.

Stop looking back at your childhood or all the failures you have had in life. God wants you to win and win big. The enemy wants you to dwell on your past hurts and failures. Take these promises of who you are from God and start to apply them every day in your life. The Bible clearly tells us about looking back.

> **Win Point:**
> You cannot have power in the present and future, holding on to the past!

> But Jesus said to him, "No one, having put his hand to the plow, and looking back, is fit for the kingdom of God" (Luke 9:62).

I must tell you: My hands are firmly clutching the plow as I steadfastly envision what He has planned for us. No looking back for me.

CHAPTER 2
TAKING YOUR THOUGHTS CAPTIVE

For as a man thinks in his heart, so is he. (Prov. 23:7)

I can still remember all the nights of abuse and plotting revenge. I was molested at home, so I took all my anger out on others outside my home. I was going to get others before they got me. All I thought about was how much I hated everyone. I hated my abuser, my parents, and my brothers and sisters. All I thought about was hate and revenge.

These are powerful words! They tell us that our thought process dictates the kind of lives we live. We either live a life that walks in mediocrity or a life that walks in victory! Being a born-again believer does not mean the enemy and the world does not influence our thinking. Have you ever been in prayer, and you start singing the lyrics to a bad song in your head? Have you ever been in church, and a bad thought pops up? Where do those thoughts come from? It is Satan pulling up old files from your past or trying to influence you today. Our childhood memories, any abuse, or past relationships will be used by the enemy to keep us from a victorious life.

You probably can remember many words spoken to you as a child:

- "You're not good enough."

- "You're never going to amount to anything."

- "Why are you not like your brother or sister?"

- "You are the reason your mom/dad and I fight."

- "It's all your fault."

You live with these words the rest of your life, unless you learn that those words are not who you are.

Here is an old lie that everyone has repeated and believed for years, "Sticks and stones may break my bones, but words will never hurt me." Most children learn this saying at an early age. I remember saying this many times as a kid as I ran around the playground at school. Here is the truth about that saying.

> *"Sticks and stones may break your bones, but words will kill you."*

If we let them, they will become who we are in life.

Words become part of our thought process and greatly influence who we are and who we are becoming. We cannot and will not win the battle of the mind unless we begin to start taking our thoughts captive and casting them out. We have the power to do so. Use it!

We cannot have the power to live a life of holiness and righteousness while thinking bad thoughts.

Our minds are like the hard drive on a computer; they store files. When we need information, we pull up the file and click on it to retrieve the information. Just like a computer user, the great deceiver is a master at pulling up files. Just like the hard drive on our computer, the mind takes all the information from our lives and stores it until it is pulled up. The enemy loves to pull up records of our past to make us feel unworthy. He loves bringing up all the past failures, hurts, trials, and tragedies that we have experienced. This is why it is so vitally important to guard our minds against the attacks of Satan. He knows that if he can influence our thinking, he can rule our hearts, causing us to live contrary to the Word of God.

Let's look at a practical way to take control of our thoughts. Whenever we get a thought that does not line up with Philippians 4:8, we know it is not from God.

> *Finally, brethren, whatsoever things are TRUE, whatsoever things are NOBLE, whatsoever things are JUST, whatsoever things are PURE, whatsoever things are LOVELY, whatsoever things are of GOOD REPORT, if there is any virtue and if there is anything praiseworthy—meditate on these things. (Phil. 4:8, emphasis added)*

If a thought enters our minds and it does not line up with this verse, it cannot be from God. As thoughts come into our mind, we need to recognize where they come from and start taking negative thoughts captive in the name of Jesus Christ. Remember,

"For as he thinks in his heart, so is he" (Prov. 23:7).

God has given us a template for our thought process. This pattern can be found in Philippians 4:8. Templates can be used for many things. In sewing, templates are used to make patterns for the item to be sown. In decorating, templates are used for painting certain figures and objects. Templates are used to manufacture many things. We use templates in life to make sure that what we are building or manufacturing is going to be the same as the original.

God has a thought process that He wants us to follow. What we think and do should line up with the template God has in His Word. If we say we are born again, washed in the blood of Jesus, then our thought process should line up with His Word.

Every thought we receive is either from above or from down below. If the thought is from below, it will not and cannot benefit us or anyone around us in any way. Satan's plan is destruction! He wants to control our thought processes. He wants to feed us negative thoughts, and he wants to bring up our past history. Along with our thought processes, he wants to control our emotions and our actions as well. Even though Satan has access to our emotions, God gives us the power to control our thoughts through Jesus Christ. Walking in victory starts by letting our thought processes be controlled by the Holy Spirit.

GOD HAS ACCESS TO:

↓   ↓   ↓

Body (Soma)	Soul (Psyche)	Spirit (Pneuma)
SIGHT SMELL HEARING TOUCHING TASTING	(THOUGHTS) THE STARTER (EMOTIONS) THE RESPONDER (ACTIONS) THE DECIDER	FAITH HOPE REVERANCE PRAYER WORSHIP

↑   ↑

SATAN HAS LIMITED ACCESS TO:

We are SPIRIT, we have a SOUL, and we live in a BODY.

> *Now may the God of peace Himself sanctify you completely; and may your whole spirit, soul, and*

> *body be preserved blameless at the coming of our Lord Jesus Christ. (1 Thess. 5:23)*

This is the battle we fight every day!

Taking our thoughts captive is a very important step in winning the spiritual battles. I challenge you to start taking back what the enemy has stolen from you. Whenever a thought enters your mind that does not line up with Philippians 4:8, you must realize that it's not coming from God. You must then take that thought captive in the name of Jesus. You pray, "In the name of Jesus Christ, I rebuke this thought. In the name of Jesus, I take this thought captive and cast it out." The Holy Spirit takes over at this point, and it's amazing how fast He takes the thought away. This is one of the greatest gifts God has given you, the power through the Holy Spirit to take your thoughts captive. You might be reading this and thinking, "Yeah right, it can't be that easy." The Word of God says, " … *Lord, even the demons are subject to us in Your name.*" *(Luke 10:17).*

> *And do not be conformed to this world, but be transformed by the renewing of your mind, that you may prove what is that good and acceptable and perfect will of God. (Rom. 12:2)*

It's only when we let God take control that we truly begin to live in the supernatural spirit of God. The world wants to pull us in the opposite direction from where Christ wants us to go. We must be very careful with everything we listen to, watch, or read.

Taking Your Thoughts Captive

The world has a great influence on our thinking. We hear young teens say, "I only listen to the beat, I don't pay attention to the words." Wrong! I remember when I was a teen listening to Rock-n-Roll music and I would say the same thing. Here is what I know: the things that go in eventually come out. I have not listened to this song in over 30 years, but I still remember the lyrics of certain songs, word for word -- confirming there is power in our thoughts. We can't win the battle and walk in victory when we watch, listen to, and do things that do not line up with God's Word. Realize we are in a battle for our thoughts and for our minds! Listen to what God's Word says about it.

> *[21] I find then a law, that evil is present with me, the one who wills to do good. [22] For I delight in the law of God according to the inward man. [23] But I see another law in my members, warring against the law of my mind, and bringing me into captivity to the law of sin which is in my members. [24] O wretched man that I am! Who will deliver me from this body of death? [25] I thank God—through Jesus Christ our Lord! So then, with the mind I myself serve the law of God, but with the flesh the law of sin. (Rom. 7:21–25)*

If you were to stop reading here, it might seem like you are fighting a losing battle. However, the great thing about serving God is that He always provides a way for victory. That's incredible! You can always win if you depend on

Him. Let's read further and find out what the rest of the story says:

> [5] *For those who live according to the flesh set their minds on the things of the flesh, but those who live according to the Spirit, the things of the Spirit.* [6] *For to be carnally minded is death, but to be spiritually minded is life and peace.* [7] *Because the carnal mind is enmity against God; for it is not subject to the law of God, nor indeed can be. (Rom. 8:5–7)*

When the Holy Spirit is active in your life, you can live in the power of God. The ability to take your thoughts captive and rebuke them is so vitally important to your walk with Christ. I encourage you to start doing that today. The more you take your thoughts captive, the easier it becomes. It will become part of your life. Stop letting the enemy control your thoughts. This is a practical way to help you take on the mind of Christ. When you start to take control of your thoughts, you are beginning the process of walking in victory.

Satan's plan has not changed since his fall from grace. It is to deceive the world, and born-again believers are included in his deception. If the great deceiver can control your thought process, he can control your life.

With every thought you reap an emotion,

With every emotion you reap an action,

With every action you establish your testimony!

CHAPTER 3
UNCONFESSED SIN

How many times in your life have you prayed, and you didn't feel like God was hearing you? How many times have you read your Bible, and the Holy Spirit did not reveal anything to you? Unconfessed sin is hindering you from winning spiritual battles. Walking around with unconfessed sin is like walking around with earplugs in your ears. It's like carrying around 200 pounds of extra weight. You can't feel the power of the Holy Spirit working in your life with unconfessed sin. You sin so often that you don't even realize that you are carrying it around. Then, you open your Bible and God wants to teach you, but sin gets in the way. You carry these sins around, and they build up and build up. You create a wall between God and you. Let's pull that wall of unconfessed sin down and enjoy walking in victory, just as God wants us to.

In the Old Testament, when the high priest would enter the Holy of Holies to offer the sacrifice for sins, the other priests would tie a rope around his ankle. If the high priest's personal sins were not properly atoned, God would strike the high priest dead. Then the other priests would have to drag his body out. In other words, the people completely relied on the work of the high priest. When the high priest emerged from the tabernacle, his appearance was a cause of much celebration and joy among the people. God is perfect, God is holy, God is pure, and God is righteous. He cannot be in the presence of sin. You must present to Him a heart that is pure and free from sin in order to experience God on a supernatural level.

Before we even open our Bible or begin to pray, we must ask God to reveal any unconfessed sin we have in our lives. Then, and only then, can we enter the presence of the almighty God. Many times, we open our Bible, and it seems like just another book. The Bible is the inspired Word of God that should always change us any time we read it.

We should not expect to be the same after we open God's Word. The Holy Spirit is alive and well and in the transformation business through the Word of God. God truly wants to change us every day through every moment we spend in the living Word.

If we confess our sins, He is faithful and just to forgive us our sins and to cleanse us from all unrighteousness. (1 John 1:9)

The Word of God is life changing whether we are ten years old, thirty-five years old, or even seventy-five years old. Once we start applying this principle to our everyday life, God's Word will come alive, and we will enjoy walking in victory. I started applying this in my life many years ago, and what a difference it has made!

You will discover that *confession* will free you up to enjoy fellowship and intimacy in the presence of your heavenly Father. It will ease your conscience and lighten your load. Don't believe that there is any sin God cannot forgive. You must understand that God wants to forgive you; that's why He sent His only begotten Son to die, be buried and resurrected for you.

> **Win Point:** Unconfessed sin makes you unprepared to win any spiritual battles!

The great news is once God reveals your sins and you ask for forgiveness, He will forgive you, never to remember your sins again. The great deceiver will bring the sins of your past up and want to make you feel like an unworthy sinner. Once you are forgiven, God never remembers your sins again. That's our awesome God; that's our God who truly has agape love.

As far as the east is from the west, So far has He removed our transgressions from us. (Ps. 103:12)

This same principle holds true for your prayer life. Before you ever go into prayer, ask God to reveal any unconfessed sin that you have in your life. Unconfessed sin hinders your prayer life, just as it does your Bible reading. To enter the presence of your Creator, you must have an unblemished heart. Prayer is the key to walking in victory. The sad truth is that many times believers don't have a powerful prayer life. Your prayer life is the single most important aspect of your spiritual walk.

Anything that hinders or detracts you from it is not good. You must take time to pray and understand that God wants to answer your prayers, but your unconfessed sin is in the way.

Prayer is how you become intimate with God. He wants that personal relationship with you through your prayer life. God speaks to you in your prayer and reflection times. Prayer is time that you set aside each day to honor and show reverence to God. This truly shows Him how much you love Him.

We may have satellite or internet television in our homes. It's great as long as we have no storms in the area. When we have a lightning storm or a storm high in the air, the satellite signal gets disrupted. This usually happens in the crucial part of a ball game. The screen goes black, and a window comes up that reads, "Searching for satellite signal or "No internet connection." Even though we have satellite or internet television, it is no good for us because we have no signal.

That is exactly how it works when we continue to pray with sin in our lives. We know that God is there, but we don't see the picture because our signal or prayers are disrupted by sin. Let's go back to the Bible verse: *"If we confess our sins, He is faithful and just to forgive us our sins and to cleanse us from all unrighteousness"* (I John 1:9).

This is a Bible verse that all believers need to hide in their hearts. Once you start practicing asking God to reveal any unconfessed sin and entering into His presence with prayers, then you can walk in victory!

CHAPTER 4
SPIRITUAL NEUTRALITY

If we are going to start winning the spiritual battles we are facing, we cannot do it being spiritually neutral. Why is it that in churches across America, the most excited people for Jesus are the new believers? Shouldn't believers who have been Christians the longest and have seen God's power and miracles in their lives be the most fired up for Jesus? I remember as a new believer, I wanted to tell everyone about Jesus. I became a "Jesus Freak" just as Cristina had called me the day I repented and recognized Jesus as my Lord and Savior. I am more excited about Jesus today because of what He has taken me through and what He has done in my family's lives. Take a look at the church you belong to. You can usually see them coming down the hall or walking in the door, the new born-again believer, walking a little faster, smiling and on fire for God, and hungry for the Word. The seasoned believer will even sometimes be annoyed because they are so excited. It should be that the person who has known Christ the longest should be the one smiling and dancing in the halls. What happened? God gave me a name for it about ten years ago before speaking for a men's conference.

I call this *spiritual neutrality or being spiritually neutral*. This is where many of our church members are today. They go to church, sing the songs, know the lingo; they even tithe, but they do not walk in victory. They walk in defeat, overcome by all the cares, and worries of the world. Life is draining every bit of spirituality out of them. They are not on fire for God. Their lives do not reflect the supernatural sovereignty of God.

Satan wants to render believers spiritually neutral; when a believer is in neutral, it's just like having your car in neutral. When a car is in neutral, the motor is still running and sometimes when you're in it, you might think you're in gear, until you press on the accelerator and realize you're not going anywhere.

> **Win Point:** You cannot win the spiritual battles when you're spiritually neutral.

Our car is no use to us in neutral just as believers are no use to God or His kingdom when they are in neutral. A car in neutral can be pushed forward, but it can also be pushed backward. This is what the Bible is referring to when it says, *"tossed to and fro"* (Eph. 4:14). A spiritually neutral believer will be tossed and pushed by the enemy. We can never stand strong when we are being tossed to and fro. We must continue to mature spiritually to be able to be strong enough to fight and win the battles.

That's the perfect deception of the evil one. If he has us spiritually neutral, we don't even know we are there because we're still playing the Christian game. If we were backsliding or in reverse, we would know that we were not doing what God wants us to do with our lives. However, when we are spiritually neutral for a long time, we might not ever know we need to get back into drive. Believers who are spiritually neutral become religious. They do everything that the church tells them to do, but they have no power in their lives. Some believers who are rendered spiritually neutral stay that way for years and years. Our churches are full of them. They are born-again believers, washed in the blood of Jesus, but ineffective for the kingdom of God. They have been believers for years and are nothing more than "pew potatoes."

In our homes, we have "couch potatoes," but in the church we have "pew potatoes." They come to church every time the doors open and do nothing when they walk out. As believers, our worship and testimony should start when we leave the church building and go home or to work. But, when we are spiritually neutral, we are no different when we walk out than when we walked in. We can't walk in power and victory when we are spiritually neutral. Supernatural living only comes when we step into the light of God, move forward, and start striving to be like Christ.

The quickest way to get out of spiritual neutrality is by asking God to forgive us for not serving Him. Begin every day in prayer, reading, and meditating on God's Holy Word. Then, ask God where we can serve. Getting involved in ministry will keep us sharp. It will keep us engaged in the kingdom of God. Become a life-giving servant! When we get involved in work for His kingdom, it's amazing how empowered we feel.

When we take our eyes off ourselves and put them on others, God supernaturally empowers us to win the spiritual battles. God will not use people who are totally consumed and focused on themselves. Jesus was the perfect example for us. Jesus was Life-giving and He was the greatest servant. He gave His very life so that you and I could have abundant life here on Earth and eternal life in heaven.

We cannot reflect Jesus if we do not serve and care for others before ourselves.

If we truly cared about others, we will be telling them about Jesus and His saving grace. The enemy does not want us to care for or share with others the goodness of who Jesus is. The enemy knows his eternal destiny is in the lake of fire, and he wants to take as many with him as possible.

When was the last time we witnessed to anyone? Spiritually neutral people do not witness to others!

The reason most people don't witness is because they don't have enough Jesus in them.

When we are spiritually neutral, our Holy Spirit tank is empty. We must keep full of His Word and prayed up in order to win the spiritual battles. If we are full the Holy Spirit, we can't help but witness and spill over into the world. Take a glass and start adding water to it; suddenly it is full. Then, when it is full it begins to spill out. The same is true in our walk as believers. We must continue to fill our spiritual tank so that we can make a difference in this dying world.

We don't have to take classes to tell other people about our children or grandchildren. When we are talking, it just comes out. Why? Because they are on the forefront of our minds and hearts. When we are full of Jesus, it will just come out.

In Chapter 1, we learned that we are light in this dark world. To be light, we must walk in the light. As we step out into the light of who Christ is, we will begin to become light. As our walk continues, we become empowered by the light so that our light can begin to shine. Our life is a mere reflection of Christ Jesus, His light reflecting on us, and our light reflecting on the world. Again, we must be full of light so it can radiate out of us. Jesus Christ Himself is the light! Jesus tells us in the Bible,

> *"You are the light of the world. A city that is set on a hill cannot be hidden. 15 Nor do they light a lamp and put it under a basket, but on a lampstand, and it gives light to all who are in the house." (Matt. 5:14–15)*

The reason most born-again believers are living powerless lives, is in the next verse:

> *"Let your light so shine before men, that they may see your good works and glorify your Father in heaven. (Matt. 5:16)*

These are very powerful words when we put them to work in our lives. Our light will not shine before men if we are spiritually neutral. If our lives are not glorifying God, we are not letting our light shine, and we will slip into darkness.

> *"Having their understanding darkened, being alienated from the life of God, because of the ignorance that is in them, because of the blindness of their heart;"* (Eph. 4:18)

I spent eight and a half years in the United States Coast Guard. I remember serving aboard the *USCG Valiant*. Our ship had to use buoys with lights, lighthouses, or navigation lights set up to guide us. Seeing the light shining through the fog or darkness has saved many lives over the years. Lights have saved many lives over the course of history. When a ship is navigating in rivers during the day, day boards are used to guide them. When navigating in the darkness of night, they use navigation lights to guide them through the waters.

Coast Guardsmen are called "the lifesavers." It is amazing because Jesus is our ultimate Lifesaver. Our jobs were to save the lives of those in danger. Many times, we would have to pull people from dangerous waters at night.

The only way we could locate them was a strobe light attached to their life jackets. Furthermore, if a boat was lost at sea or capsized, we were able to locate them when they shot the flair gun, which emitted a bright light. Light is very important in emergencies.

Spiritual Neutrality

I remember serving during "Mariel Boatlift" in 1980, when Fidel Castro opened the flood gates from Cuba. Thousands of Cubans fled the tyranny of a socialist dictator. Most made it across safely, but many lost their lives because we could not locate them, and they drifted out to sea to die. Some were hit by boats, and some sank in boats that were not seaworthy. If they'd had emergency lights, many could have been saved.

The same is true in our world today. Many lives are drifting out to sea and getting hit by life and the evil one. There are many people who need to see a light. Our world is dying and going to hell because not enough lights are shining. Start walking in victory today and be that shining light in the world. We don't have to know all the Bible verses or be a great speaker.

We need to trust God and be available for service. We will need to top off our Jesus tank every day, staying full and letting our light overflow into this dark, dying world. We must be full of Jesus for Jesus to come out. Most believers walk around half full of Jesus and half full of the world. When they get a chance to witness, the world comes out. We need to fill up daily with the Word and be fully prayed up. We can't allow the enemy to keep us spiritually neutral.

We can't walk in victory when we're spiritually neutral.

We must get involved in what God is doing! Get involved in ministry, doing the work of the ministry. We are saved to serve. God did not send His Son to pay the price for our sin so that we can just sit on the sideline.

It's time to get out of neutral, get in gear, and start moving forward. God wants us to continually move forward in our relationship with Him and the ministry that He has given us here on Earth to do.

The Great Commission should be our focus as we move forward. It is time to move forward in our prayer life, in our Bible time, and in the ministry to which He has called us. Believers have been rendered spiritually neutral and ineffective for His kingdom. That's exactly where Satan wants us to be.

Who is usually the most excited about what God is doing in their lives? New believers!

Who is telling the most people about Jesus? New believers! Who is the hungriest for the Word? New believers!

Who has the most positive attitude? New believers!

Who is usually walking around with a large smile on their faces? New believers!

What happens to a believer's joy and hunger for the Word? This is where the enemy comes in and renders most believers spiritually neutral. This could happen any time after our profession of faith. Satan cannot touch our souls, but he can influence us and keep us stuck in neutral. We might still go to church, maybe we still tithe, we sing the songs, we know the church lingo, but we are not winning the spiritual battles. We are not being a bold witness for the kingdom of God.

Spiritually neutral believers are permeating churches across America. They play the game but are not walking in victory. They may even get annoyed by new believers who are on fire for God! We can see them every Sunday,

Spiritual Neutrality

walking around with no joy in their lives. Everything is a struggle for them, even serving God. How can we avoid this? Discipleship! Find a mentor, an accountability partner! Find believers who are walking out their faith, not just talking about a godly life, and ask them to disciple us. The Bible says, *"Yet you do not have because you do not ask" (James 4:2)*. If we want an accountability/discipleship partner, pray and seek one out so we have help growing spiritually. God expects us to live a godly life.

"People do what is inspected not what is expected."

An accountability partner is valuable in helping us with our spiritual disciples and win the spiritual battles we will face.

> *9 Two are better than one, because they have a good reward for their labor. 10 For if they fall, one will lift up his companion. But woe to him who is alone when he falls, For he has no one to help him up. 11 Again, if two lie down together, they will keep warm; But how can one be warm alone? 12 Though one may be overpowered by another, two can withstand him. And a threefold cord is not quickly broken. (Eccles. 4:9–12)*

They will help us when we start to become spiritually neutral. They will encourage us and motivate us and sometimes show us tough love to get us back on track.

It's biblical that we seek out and find a mentor and stick to him or her like a shadow.

Most believers are not pouring their lives into one another. When someone becomes a new believer, he or she should be immediately paired up with a mentor or accountability partner to help him/her walk with Jesus Christ. They need to be fed appropriate spiritual food, just as a newborn needs to be fed liquids.

If you are a new believer, baby believer, or feel like you're spiritually neutral, start praying for a discipleship partner. Go to your pastor or someone in leadership in your church and ask for help in finding a partner.

> *[1] And I, brethren, could not speak to you as to spiritual people but as to carnal, as to babes in Christ. [2] I fed you with milk and not with solid food; for until now you were not able to receive it, and even now you are still not able. (1 Cor. 3:1–2)*

New believers need to be nourished when they are babies in Christ. As believers grow, they must be continually fed the right food. Babies can only digest puréed foods, such as mashed up vegetables, fruit, and juices. Once they have grown, they can eat solid foods. If a newborn baby looks the same way and acts the same way a year later, we would call a doctor because we would know that there is a problem. Yet, many believers are walking around the same as they have been for years and still no growth. As a believer, we must be fed the right food to grow. We cannot expect to walk in victory when we are the same year after year. We must see spiritual growth in our life. If we are leaving church the same as we came in week after week, there is a problem. If we are in the Word and staying the same, we are not allowing God to change us.

> *¹² For though by this time you ought to be teachers, you need someone to teach you again the first principles of the oracles of God; and you have come to need milk and not solid food. ¹³ For everyone who partakes only of milk is unskilled in the word of righteousness, for he is a babe. ¹⁴ But solid food belongs to those who are of full age, that is, those who by reason of use have their senses exercised to discern both good and evil. (Heb. 5:12–14)*

This is not happening in most churches today. If your church has a ministry like this, you are blessed. If your church does not have a mentorship or accountability program, pray for God to bring someone into your life to mentor you or someone who you can mentor. The best scenario is for us to have a mentor and to be mentoring someone. This keeps us sharp, fresh, and on fire for God. This will help you win spiritual battles.

This is what living the empowered life is all about. Many churches are missing out by not having a mentor or accountability program. We can keep fellow brothers and sisters from becoming spiritually neutral by helping them grow in Christ, grow in the Word, and serve in ministry. New babes in Christ need to see and hear what

God has done in the life of their mentor or accountability partners. The forty-year-old believer should be mentoring someone younger, and the thirty-year-old believer should be mentoring someone younger.

This is true discipleship, which reflects Paul's writings to Titus. This should be the standard operating procedure for every evangelical, empowered, living church. This is where the empowered mature Christian life comes from.

The way to stay on fire for God is to stay active in His kingdom ministry.

Invest your time and effort in others' lives, knowing that this is commanded in the Word of God.

> *[1] But as for you, speak the things which are proper for sound doctrine: [2] that the older men be sober, reverent, temperate, sound in faith, in love, in patience; [3] the older women likewise, that they be reverent in behavior, not slanderers, not given to much wine, teachers of good things—[4] that they admonish the young women to love their husbands, to love their children, [5] to be discreet, chaste, homemakers, good, obedient to their own husbands, that the word of God may not be blasphemed. [6] Likewise, exhort the young men to be sober-minded, [7] in all things showing yourself to be a pattern of good works; in doctrine showing integrity, reverence, incorruptibility, [8] sound speech that cannot be condemned, that one who*

is an opponent may be ashamed, having nothing evil to say of you. (Titus 2:1–8)

CHAPTER 5
BE AVAILABLE

God is not looking for ability; He is looking for availability. To truly walk in victory, we must be available to follow God's calling for our lives. Most born-again believers live their whole lives never knowing what God wants them to do. They get so caught up in life that they miss knowing what God's intentions are for their lives. The world can get them so caught up in it that they start to become like the world. The Bible clearly tells us to be in the world but not of the world. Most of the time, when God calls on us, we are so busy that we are not available to hear Him or respond to Him. We need to get rid of all the distractions of life that hinder our availability to follow our Lord and Savior's call.

> [18] *And Jesus, walking by the Sea of Galilee, saw two brothers, Simon called Peter, and Andrew his brother, casting a net into the sea; for they were fishermen.* [19] *Then He said to them, "Follow Me, and I will make you fishers of men."* (Matt. 4:18–19)

This is true availability to the calling of our Lord and Savior. This should be our response to the call of God. Notice, there were no hesitations at all!

> *"They immediately left their nets and followed Him)* "Matt. 4:20).

Can you believe this? Immediately! It is so amazing to know that although they knew exactly who He was, they did not know the exact ministry He was calling them into. Yet they followed Him.

Sometimes God calls us just to see what our response is. He wants to see if we are going to say, "yes" or "maybe later" or "no, no, not me." The same thing happened again with James and John:

> [21] *Going on from there, He saw two other brothers, James the son of Zebedee, and John his brother, in the boat with Zebedee their father, mending their nets. He called them,* [22] *and immediately they left the boat and their father and followed Him.* (Matt. 4:21–22)

Now imagine what their father had to say when this Man comes up and calls his two sons to drop everything and follow Him. What would you tell your sons? I know as a father I would not want my son to rush into anything without counting the costs. Being available and answering the call of God are not always popular with your family members. They will not understand. However, if my son told me, "Dad, I know this is God calling me," I would not have a problem with it.

God wants only our obedience, and that means being available to the call of God. Obedience is the number one thing God wants from all His children. He wants obedience more than sacrifice.

> *"So, Samuel said: . . . As in obeying the voice of the LORD? Behold, to obey is better than sacrifice"* (1 Sam. 15:22).

If we do not make ourselves available to God, He will use someone else. God's plan will get accomplished with or without us. Walking in victory comes from being in God's will and His plan for our lives. Don't miss out on one of the greatest blessings God wants to share with you.

I remember being awakened by God in July of 2001; I went into prayer, and God revealed to me I would be in full-time ministry in thirteen months. This started a number of supernatural events that happened over the next thirteen months that I must share with you. The reason I am sharing this is so God can get all the glory and to show you how God can use any vessel that is available.

> **Win Point:**
> The will of God will never take you where the grace of God will not provide for you.

We had been members of Cielo Vista Church in El Paso, Texas, for six years. Cielo Vista was exploding; we went from 600 to over 1,200 members in about twelve months. God was moving in our church, and we were comfortable there. We invited many of our friends, and they joined our church. But we realized it was not about what we wanted; but it was about what God wanted for our lives. God was moving in a miraculous way. The Holy Spirit kept putting a burden on my heart to leave our church and find out where God wanted me to serve.

My wife, Cristina, and I really did not want to leave our church. It was not an easy move, leaving comfortable surroundings to pursue the place in which God wanted us to serve. God was directing our family to a church that we had visited two other times and were not really excited about. In our previous visits, the people were not welcoming and were cold toward us. Cristina and I felt the same way each time we visited. However, when we stepped foot into that church the next time, we knew it was our new home.

I knew the Lord was calling me to lead men, so I set up a meeting with Pastor Rix Tillman. He informed me that he had been praying for God to send someone to start a men's ministry. I thank God for Pastor Rix believing in me and allowing me the opportunity to lead the men of Exciting Immanuel Church. God truly used him to guide and teach me in my early years of ministry. God is so awesome! I became the men's director and with the guidance of Pastor Rix as a mentor and led by the Holy Spirit, we were off and running.

We witnessed a great movement of the Holy Spirit among the men at Exciting Immanuel Church. Men were saved, men were on fire for God, and marriages were being put back together. God was moving in a huge way! We had something special, and I thank God for that experience. Men still call me today to talk about how God moved in that ministry. I did not realize it at the time, but God was using me in this ministry as a stepping stone for something bigger.

About two years later, I knew God was calling me into full-time ministry. I immediately told Pastor Rix and the leaders of GAME (God's Army of Men Excelling), the name of our men's group. Most were receptive to where the Holy Spirit was leading me, but I had some people tell me I was already in full-time ministry. Some people tried to tell me where God was really leading me, but I knew God had bigger plans for my life. I learned a valuable lesson: *when God speaks, don't listen to others*. God knows what is best for you even though other people may want what is best for them. They don't know the whole picture or what God's will is for our lives. God already has our lives planned out for His glory and His kingdom. We must not let someone else steal the gift God has chosen for us!

In my career, I was a sales manager for a digital imaging company. I had previously been the president of a company and owned two other businesses. I was also doing motivational speaking and consulting. The company I was working for as sales manager was growing at a very fast pace, and things were going very well. Cristina had been working for the same company for twenty-three years and was vice-president of marketing. Our champions, (our children) Beau and Mia, were in a Christian school, and we were living what the world calls, "the good life."

Three years prior to my calling, we had purchased the home of our dreams. We had built a beautiful custom swimming pool complete with hot tub and waterfall and we drove matching Cadillacs. But when God truly calls, your future might be changed.

It was September, and I was getting ready to go to church. Cristina served on the multi-media ministry team for our church and had to leave before the rest of us on Sunday mornings for the early services. I stayed back to make sure the champions were up, fed, and ready for church. I taught the new members class every Sunday morning, but that Sunday was different. I received a call from Cristina, and she informed me that the guest speaker for our week-long revival was preaching about the same things I had been saying for years. She said that I should get over there as quickly as possible. As soon as I walked in the sanctuary that morning, it was like I had known this man my entire life.

The evangelist was preaching the exact things that I had been reading, studying, and teaching about: living free, experiencing the power of the Holy Spirit, and winning the spiritual battles. He was preaching about living holy and righteous lives. As soon as he had finished preaching, he walked down the aisle where I was sitting, held out his hand and said, "God has sent me here for you." He proceeded to tell me that I would be in full time ministry soon. For the first time in my life, I was almost speechless. I knew he was sent by God for me. He was at our church for a week-long revival.

That week, I was attending a convention in Albuquerque, New Mexico, four hours away and had a room there every night, but the Holy Spirit kept drawing me back. I would drive home every night to hear the

Word God had for me and then wake up early the next day and drive back to Albuquerque. I had a room at a five-star resort and never slept there one night. God's Word is much better than any resort! I was then invited to preach at his church in Oklahoma. I had only preached once in my life prior to that! I had been teaching for years but not preaching. God began to open doors for me to preach that were never open before.

Then things began to happen. In November, God woke me up in the middle of the night and told me that we needed to sell our house. Not only did He tell me to sell it, but He also told me the price. My first reaction was, "God, why didn't you wake up Cristina and tell her to sell our house? Why do I have to tell her? More than that, what will I tell her?" It took me two weeks to get the nerve to tell Cristina what God had told me. She listened calmly and then went ballistic! She informed me that the God she worshiped was not the same God I was talking to! She told me this was the home of our dreams; we had talked about raising our champions and grand champions there. She said there was no way that she was selling this home! God then told me to let Him handle Cristina. This was one battle that I gladly let Him have.

I was asked by a friend of mine, Gary Wilcox, to preach at his church in Ft. Hancock, Texas. After I preached, he asked me to preach again, and I ended up preaching there on and off for about two months. The whole time I was preaching there, I did not know that Gary was going to resign.

In May, he resigned from the church. He asked me if I would mind preaching in Ft. Hancock until they found an interim or full-time pastor. Anytime I can preach God's Word I will, and so I agreed. By that time, it was June of 2002. I was in the shower, and I said to God, "God, you said I would be in ministry in thirteen months. Well, it has been eleven months, and I am not getting any direction." Then I asked God, "God, please show me something!" I finished showering, and about ten minutes later, the phone started ringing. God told me that it was Craig Miller on the phone.

Cristina walked up to me and said that the call was for me. I already knew who it was. Sure enough, it was Craig asking me if I would be interim pastor in Ft. Hancock. *God is in control!* Ten minutes after I prayed, God showed me that He is still in control of everything. I met with the leadership of the church and became their interim pastor.

By July of 2002, twelve months into ministry, the Holy Spirit was revealing many things to me. I knew my time in the business world was ending. I had lost my desire to continue in the business world. I knew it was time to let go and let God. It was all about stepping out on faith and trusting God. He had been telling me to trust Him.

I woke up on Monday and went down to my office, knowing this was it. I stepped into my boss's office and informed him that I was giving my two-week notice. He was shocked that I would give up "all this," as he put it, to go into the ministry. We talked for about an hour, and when I left his office, I felt so relieved. I knew from then on it was all up to God.

After leaving my job, we noticed that our lifestyle had not changed, even though our income had been significantly reduced. Cristina and I did not know how the bills were being paid, but we continued to pray about where God was leading us. We didn't understand things, but it wasn't for us to understand.

Two days later, we were pulling out of the parking lot of the church when the phone rang. It was Craig Miller asking me to become the full-time pastor. That is so God! Isn't He wonderful?

Do you see how it was my availability to God's calling and being in tune with His plan for my life that allowed this to happen? When we stop living for ourselves and start living for Christ, that's when He takes over.

We can't begin the process of walking in victory if we are not available.

God works in such a supernatural way. The whole time God was calling me to full-time ministry, I just knew it was to expand our men's ministry. We already had chapters in four churches, and things were going great.

We had two men's days that saw over two thousand men come and many making decisions. I just knew men's ministry was my calling. Notice I said, "I knew." If we are going to win the spiritual battle, we must understand God's ways are not our ways, even when we want it our way.

> [8] *"For My thoughts are not your thoughts,*
> *Nor are your ways My ways," says the LORD.*
> [9] *"For as the heavens are higher than the earth,*
> *So are My ways higher than your ways,*
> *And My thoughts than your thoughts.*
> (Isa. 55:8–9)

To wrap up this chapter of my life, I was ordained pastor on September 2, 2002; thirteen months and two days after God woke me up that night in June 2001. It was tough leaving the men at Immanuel behind, but we knew God was leading us to Ft. Hancock.

We did not move there until May of 2003. Ft. Hancock is forty-five miles east of El Paso, Texas, so I was commuting back and forth every day. In January of 2003, Cristina woke up one morning and informed me that God had given her release on the house, and she was ready to sell it. She knew God wanted us to sell. God also told us we would sell the house ourselves, and we would not need to put up a sign or anything like that. The first couple who looked at it was a couple Cristina had worked with in the past, Charlie and Araceli Arellano. They knew one of our neighbors and heard we were selling. They came to look at the house the very next day and bought it for the exact price God had given me! It is amazing what God can do when we let Him.

The most exciting part was the night we signed the contract. After the contract was signed, the Holy Spirit told me to witness to the couple who bought our house, so I began to tell them about the Lord. The Holy Spirit moved in their hearts that night, and they accepted Jesus Christ! Hallelujah! What if we had not sold the house and just rented it?

Charlie is now serving as the Executive Pastor at Cielo Vista Church in El Paso and touching many lives for the kingdom. Talk about a divine appointment!

Be Available

God's plan is always bigger than we know.

He knew we needed to sell the house so this precious couple could come to know Christ. Now they are in church and serving the Lord. As I stated before, God's ways are not our ways!

During the next two years, God moved in a big way, and we saw the church grow and many people saved and baptized. We were excited about our first church and the opportunity to serve God.

I want to rewind to about six months prior to Cristina and me accepting God's call to our first church. One night in March of 2002, Cristina woke me up in the middle of the night. She told me that the Holy Spirit had woken her up and told her I needed to witness to Dee, my father, one more time. I was a bit hesitant, knowing that my father had Parkinson's and Alzheimer's diseases. This is the same father who had been physically, mentally, and verbally abusive to me my whole childhood. He was eighty-one and in a nursing home. But even in my humanly resistant state, I told her if God told you that, then book a flight for me – which she promptly did, even though I really did not want to go.

Upon arriving in Louisiana on a Sunday evening, I went to visit Dee in the nursing home. He was totally unaware of his surroundings and anyone who came to visit him. I was really perplexed that God would wake Cristina up in the middle of the night and have me fly down to Louisiana for this. I had to keep reminding myself of Isaiah 55:8 that says, *'For My thoughts are not your thoughts, Nor are your ways My ways,' says the Lord."*

I began praying, "God, I need you to show up because I have told many people what my wife had said, and things are not looking good."

It was Monday and I went back to the nursing home early in the morning to find Dee in the same shape as the day before. I decided to take him out of the home, bring him back to where he grew up, and have lunch with him. After spending the day with Dee and not seeing any signs of his mind clearing to talk to him about God, I brought him back to the nursing home. I felt a little uneasy with the way things were turning out and really didn't anticipate there would be a change before I flew out Wednesday morning. I felt the Holy Spirit keep telling me, "It's already done. It's already done, it's already done" I drove to my mother's house thinking, I don't see anything happening, but keep reminding myself of Isaiah 55:9, *"For as the heavens are higher than the earth, So are My ways higher than your ways, And My thoughts than your thoughts."*

I did what every other man of God would do when God speaks, I called my wife Cristina, to give her a report on the day and tell her what I believed the Lord was telling me. She asked me, "Why did you call me? If the Lord is telling you, it's already done, then it's already done." She was not seeing what I was seeing.

Tuesday morning rolled around. After spending time in prayer and the Word of God, I returned to the home to see Dee. This morning was different. As I walked into his room, he was sitting in his chair. I placed my Bible on his bed, and he immediately looked up and with a clear voice said these words: "Is there something you want to read me out of the Bible? What?" This is my dad asking me about the Bible. His speech was clear and so was his mind! For the next forty-five minutes, Dee and I had a conversation we had never had before.

The conversation covered many facets of his life, church, and religion. I asked him if he would like to accept Jesus Christ as his Lord and Savior. He responded with a definite, "Yes." I had the privilege of leading my father to the Lord, even though he had Parkinson's and Alzheimer's disease. We won the spiritual victory! What a miracle from almighty God! God cleared his mind and opened his heart to the gospel. Hallelujah! Also, it was the first time my dad had ever told me, "I love you." God is still in the miracle business.

Before I flew back to El Paso the next morning, I stopped by the home to say good-bye to Dee. It would be our final good-bye here on earth. As he shuffled his way to eat breakfast, I whispered to the nurse, "Ask my dad where he would go if he died today. As I was following him and the nurse down the hall, he raised his right hand with all the strength he could muster and said, "Heaven." Praise God! Praise God!

I drove away with tears running down my face and praising God for His saving grace. Needless to say, I called Cristina to tell her and thank her for being available to hear God's voice and being obedient to His calling.

Dee died six months after I led him to the Lord. God's timing is so great. We went back to Louisiana to attend my father's funeral, and I was asked to do the eulogy. We were supposed to leave the next morning after the funeral to go back to El Paso, but God had different plans. From the time we arrived, I told Cristina I was ready to get back to Texas. You see, when I surrendered to the ministry, I prayed to God and said, "I will go anywhere in the world to serve you, but I do not want to go back to southern Louisiana." Every day I woke up wanting to leave and go home to west Texas.

It was Thursday morning, and I was ready to leave. The Holy Spirit woke me up, and I was compelled to get in our car. I told our son, Beau, "Let's go for a ride." We started driving through the area where I grew up. This time was different; I started seeing the area through God's eyes and not my feelings. God began to speak to me and tell me it's time to come home. This cannot be happening! I prayed, "I love the desert, the mountains, and the culture of west Texas, God. What about the church?"

The next morning, the same thing happened. Beau and I began to drive, and God was calling me like never before to come back and start a new church in my hometown. But what will Cristina say? Her whole family is in El Paso. She told me repeatedly she would not leave the west Texas area. She loves the desert. I cried out, "God, why didn't You tell her first? Why do I have to break the news to her?"

God was dealing with me big time, and I started getting a vision for Ascension Parish.

It was Saturday, and Cristina was wondering what was going on. I was so adamant about leaving all week, but now I was stalling to stay. She never said a word about it, though. We ended up leaving Sunday afternoon. As we headed down I-10 West, I told Cristina I had something to tell her. I braced myself for a major negative response. I told her what God, through the working of

His Holy Spirit, had impressed on my heart. I told her, "I believe God is calling us back to Gonzales to start a church." As soon as those words rolled off of my tongue, she responded, "I believe He is too!" I could not believe this! Again, God amazed me! Cristina went on to explain how the Holy Spirit had been dealing with her all week about moving to start a new church in Gonzales.

We immediately agreed that if this is what God wanted from us, we were going to be available and willing. God was compelling us into the process of leaving Texas and heading to Louisiana. After much prayer and fasting, we knew it was time. I informed the church I would be leaving and starting a new work in Louisiana effective February 1, 2005. Cristina turned in her resignation from the only place she had ever worked. She started at her job when she was eighteen, and now twenty-five years later, she was following God's call. She gave it all up to trust God for our future. Beau was in the tenth grade; Mia was in first grade. We wanted them to finish the school year. God kept telling us to go now! He opened so many doors that would not have been open if we had not been obedient.

"You have to remember that partial obedience and delayed obedience is disobedience!"

To have supernatural faith, we must step out to where only God can provide for us.

Supernatural faith comes from supernatural testing! Supernatural testing comes from supernatural circumstances!

This was definitely a supernatural circumstance.

I had only been ordained for a little over two years, and God was calling me to start a church. My first thought was, *I am not worthy or prepared.* Then I thought, *Neither was Moses or many of the other men in the Bible, who God called.*

Then I quoted scripture to God. I said, "God, Your Word says, *"But Jesus said to them, 'A prophet is not without honor except in his own country, among his own relatives, and in his own house'"* (Mark 6:4).

The Holy Spirit spoke to me and said, "You're not Jesus. Just go! We left Texas on February 11 and headed for the land of the great unknown. With the help of my brother, Bert and some dear friends Johnny and Georgia Schuller; we headed East with two Penske trucks, a suburban, and a pick-up with a cattle trailer. No income, no church, just faith in the Maker of Miracles. We were so excited to see what God would do with and in our lives.

Our first service was February 14, 2005, in the den of our rental home where my first cousin, Amy, let us live until we were established. That was another blessing from God.

We had four people at that service: Cristina, our two children, and me! Wow, we were rolling! The next Sunday my mother, Ella Rose, (for whom I had prayed for fourteen years gave her life to Jesus Christ in October of 2004 after my dad's funeral, another miracle from God) came over to our home. Along with my mother, my niece, came with her mother and her two children, Soon we had ten people coming, and we were running out of room.

God opened a small 900-square-foot office space for $600 per month. We did not have the money, so the landlord gave us the first month free. My brother, who had started coming to our church, paid for the second month. The Rock Church held its first official service on Resurrection Sunday, March 27, 2005. We had twenty-two people in attendance. We were so excited to have a church home, fifty metal chairs that cost us $700.00 (though we only had $600.00 to start this new work), and a small sound system. But we had our faith in almighty God and were led by the Holy Spirit.

Our friends, the Fayards from Oklahoma, showed up and blessed us with $2,000 to help with expenses. God was already providing for His church.

We started to grow and see people saved and baptized. It was all a "God thing." Lives were being touched and changed, and God was moving in His church. We were in that building for two years. Then God did a wonderful thing and provided us with five acres of land, sprawling with oaks trees. What a blessing! We added on to an old Quonset hut to create a 2,700-square-foot building.

The renovation and addition costs us $96,000. God spoke to me and told me that the building would be paid off when we put the key in the door. He told me to stand before the congregation and let them know what He said. God is so good and faithful. He deserves all the praise and glory! Stepping out on faith and trusting God will help us win all our spiritual battles. Being available for

God is the key to winning the battles. We moved in and our building was paid for.

God moved in an unbelievable way at The Rock in the sixteen years we pastored the church. We saw hundreds of people saved and baptized, people surrendering to the ministry and the name of God being exalted, just from being available. We experienced a mighty movement of God and reached many people in our community, that's a far cry from four people in the den of a rented home.

I have since stepped down from leading the church we planted because of losing a battle. The story will be in my next book on "Restoration." We will all have some losses in our lives, but through repentance and restoration and following the steps in this book, we can win again.

When we make ourselves available, God steps in and provides the power to help us win our spiritual battles. To live in victory, we must be available to God's calling. We must be willing to give it all up for a cause greater than our own. Being available allows God to work in our lives and further His kingdom according to His plan. Most of the time, we want to fit God's plan into ours. We will never know the awesomeness of God by doing that. Are you willing to be available? I am so glad we were!

CHAPTER 6
I AM NOT MY OWN

What is holding you back from a deep, rewarding relationship with your Creator? There are many things that can hold you back. God wants you to let everything go and let Him start to be Lord in your life. He knows more than you know, is better at finances than you are, is better at relationships than you are, knows more about raising children than you do, has a greater knowledge of business than you do, has more vision for the future than you do, knows more about health than you do, knows exactly what the future holds for you, and much more than you do. Why not let go and let Him?

To truly live with supernatural faith, you must give it all to Him.

I am always reminded of the song, "I Surrender All." It's such a beautiful song with wonderful words. Many people love that song and sing it. But I must admit, a majority of believers sing it like this, "I surrender all" and all the while they are really saying, "I surrender some." What they are really singing is, "I surrender all, but not my finances. I surrender all, but not my life. I surrender all, but not my career." Do you get the picture? God wants it all!

Until you give it all, you cannot and will not live in power. The more you surrender to God, the more faith you show in Him as Lord.

This is contrary to what the world wants you to believe. In the world, the more you control things, the more power you have. Someone once said, "Absolute power corrupts absolutely." The one thing that holds a lot of people back from accepting Jesus Christ as their Lord and Savior is the innate trait of wanting to be the *boss*. Most believers never experience the awesome life that God wants them to live because they still want to be boss of their lives. Many believers say, "Let go and let God," but they don't live what they say.

> **Win Point:**
> Walking in victory only comes from realizing, "I am not my own; I was bought with a price."

In reality, there is freedom in obedience! God does not want our sacrifice; He wants our obedience. It's like we are in a tug-of-war with God over every aspect of our lives. We should not fight God in the things He has given us or allowed us to have. You wonder why you are so tired most of the time; it's your constant struggle over what you want to control.

I Am Not My Own

Freedom comes from total surrender to God.

This frees us from the everyday burdens and lets God be Lord and Savior of our lives. This is exactly where God wants to be in your walk with Him. He wants your every burden and trouble. His Word tells you to give them to Him.

> *"Casting all your care upon Him, for He cares for you" (I Pet. 5:7).*

Sometimes you feel like the weight of the world is upon you. What are you holding onto right now in your life that is keeping you from the close relationship with God? Take a minute and write down on a sheet of paper what you have not given to God. God wants you to stop worrying and start living. Give it to God, He is big enough to handle it. To win spiritual battles, you have to give it all to God.

God cares enough for you to take your burdens and give you peace.

> [25] *"Therefore I say to you, do not worry about your life, what you will eat or what you will drink; nor about your body, what you will put on. Is not life more than food and the body more than clothing?* [26] *Look at the birds of the air, for they neither sow nor reap nor gather into barns; yet your heavenly Father feeds them. Are you not*

of more value than they? ²⁷ *Which of you by worrying can add one cubit to his stature?*

²⁸ *"So why do you worry about clothing? Consider the lilies of the field, how they grow: they neither toil nor spin;* ²⁹ *and yet I say to you that even Solomon in all his glory was not arrayed like one of these.* ³⁰ *Now if God so clothes the grass of the field, which today is, and tomorrow is thrown into the oven, will He not much more clothe you, O you of little faith?*

³¹ *"Therefore do not worry, saying, 'What shall we eat?' or 'What shall we drink?' or 'What shall we wear?'* ³² *For after all these things the Gentiles seek. For your heavenly Father knows that you need all these things.* ³³ *But seek first the kingdom of God and His righteousness, and all these things shall be added to you.* ³⁴ *Therefore do not worry about tomorrow, for tomorrow will worry about its own things. Sufficient for the day is its own trouble.* (Matt. 6:25–34)

When God says, "Let go," He really means it. The only way you can live the empowered life is by letting God be your Lord. He knows all the potholes that lay ahead of you on the road of life. He is the Master Navigator.

When He is at the controls, you will have a total peace and a fullness of joy you have never experienced before.

This is a supernatural feeling that can only come from God. It's knowing everything is going to be all right because of God's sovereignty. The sovereignty of God should be prevalent in your life every day. You say He is sovereign, but do you live like He is? The way you live should reveal the sovereignty of your Lord and Savior.

Native hunters have a clever way of trapping monkeys. They hollow out a coconut and place fruit in the coconut.

It is only a matter of time before an unsuspecting monkey swings by and smells the aroma of this delicious piece of fruit. The monkey will search around and discover the fruit is hidden inside the coconut. The monkey will slip his hand through the hole in the coconut and grab the fruit and try to pull his hand back through the hole. Of course, the monkey's hand filled with the fruit will not come out; it's too big to get through the hole. The persistent monkey continues to pull and pull, never realizing the danger he is in. While the monkey struggles with the fruit, the hunters just walk up and capture the monkey. All he had to do was let go of the fruit, and he would not have been captured. But the monkey wanted the sweet, tangy fruit more than he wanted his freedom. The monkey could have saved his life if he had just let go of the fruit.

Sadly, we choose not to let go of our fruit and let God control our lives. It never occurs to the monkey that he cannot have both the fruit and his freedom. It seldom occurs to believers they can't have what the world offers and live the powerful life God wants them to live. The world sets traps for you and me, just like the hunters. It could be the success trap, the money trap, or the prestige trap. The world appears delicious, and the aroma smells so good sometimes. Don't fall for it! Don't spend your whole life trying to pull your fruit out of the coconut. Your life is not your own...let go and let God!

Don't be like the rich young ruler in the Bible.

> *[16] Now behold, one came and said to Him, "Good Teacher, what good thing shall I do that I may have eternal life?"*
>
> *[17] So He said to him, "Why do you call Me good? No one is good but One, that is, God. But if you want to enter into life, keep the commandments."*
>
> *[18] He said to Him, "Which ones?"*
>
> *Jesus said, " 'You shall not murder,' 'You shall not commit adultery,' 'You shall not steal,' 'You shall not bear false witness,' [19] 'Honor your father and your mother,' and, 'You shall love your neighbor as yourself.' "*
>
> *[20] The young man said to Him, "All these things I have kept from my youth. What do I still lack?"*
>
> *[21] Jesus said to him, "If you want to be perfect, go, sell what you have and give to the poor, and*

you will have treasure in heaven; and come, follow Me."

²² But when the young man heard that saying, he went away sorrowful, for he had great possessions. (Matt. 19:16–22)

CHAPTER 7
FIRSTFRUITS

Here is an acrostic to follow:

F — *First thing in the morning*
I — *Invest time alone with God*
R — *Read God's Word*
S — *Seek His Face*
T — *Thank God for another day*

F — *Fellowship with God*
R — *Recognize the Lord's Sovereignty*
U — *Understand His Love*
I — *Inspiration from Scripture*
T — *Trust God Enough to Follow His Guidance*

It was once said, and I repeat it almost daily: "Your success is hidden in your daily routine." This is true in every aspect of our lives. Whether we are in business for ourselves, an employee, a student, a homemaker, in the ministry, and so forth, our success in that field will be determined by what we do daily. Our spiritual walk is no different! To have victory in our lives and to have a supernatural relationship with God, we must give God our time and our firstfruits.

> *For on My holy mountain, on the mountain height of Israel," says the Lord God, "there all the house of Israel, all of them in the land, shall serve Me; there I will accept them, and there I will require your offerings and the firstfruits of your sacrifices, together with all your holy things. (Ezek. 20:40)*

> *The firstfruits of your grain and your new wine and your oil, and the first of the fleece of your sheep, you shall give him. (Deut. 18:4)*

Not everyone in today's culture has grain, new wine, or oil, but everyone has the same twenty-four hours in a day. We can give God our firstfruits in the morning. One thing I have learned over the years:

People will find the time and money to do the things they really *want* to do.

If we want to live a life of spiritual victory over the devil, we must give God our firstfruits in the morning and begin thinking like Christ as outlined in Chapter 2.

Firstfruits are when we first wake up in the morning and we aside time to be alone with God to get to know Him through His Word and prayer. God does not like leftovers! He wants our firstfruits in the morning. Our minds are most receptive in the morning.

Firstfruits

God wants you to give yourself to Him before you give yourself to the world.

According to those who study our *circadian rhythms*, there are two times during the day our brains are most alert and receptive to incoming signals. The sharpest our minds will be is when we first wake up in the morning. This is why we should go straight into prayer and reading, meditating and studying God's Word. The second time is between 7 p.m. to 9 p.m., when we prepare ourselves for sleep.

Have you ever noticed how many things happen when you get up early ready to give God your firstfruits in the morning? The dog needs to be let out, children come in unexpectedly, you get the urge to turn on the television, a chore comes to mind that you should have taken care of yesterday. You walk into the kitchen to get a cup of coffee, and you have dishes in the sink that need to be washed or trash that needs to be taken out.

> **Win Point:**
> God does not want your leftovers, He wants your firstfruits.

If you begin to put off your firstfruits time, you never get around to it.

We were created to have fellowship with God. God wants it, and you need it. God wants the firstfruits of your time, talents, and treasures.

Prayer is a vital part of your firstfruits time. Let me share a quick story about prayer:

"Six hours of prayer, are you kidding me?" That was my first reaction to our church's new prayer ministry scheduled from 9 a.m. to 3 p.m. on Saturday. We could come and go as we liked, but because I was the men's director, I felt I should stay for one or two hours. The first Saturday, I was ready to give my all for one hour. We met at 9 a.m. and began to pray.

Before I knew it, someone said, "We will see you next week," and it was 3 p.m. Wow, I could not believe it! I had experienced God in a whole new way. By the second or third hour, I had stepped into the Presence of my almighty God. It was a whole different dimension I had never experienced before. It was a supernatural experience with God. I had just prayed for six hours. A pastor once told me that God is "intoxicating." To tell you the truth, I thought that was a little strange. But I understood what He was talking about that day. I felt like I was on a "high" I could not explain.

I could not wait for next Saturday. The more I went, the more I wanted to go. It was an incredible time in my life.

If you want powerful supernatural prayer, it takes time. You must spend a quality and a quantity amount of time with God. Five minutes in prayer will not give you power in your life. When you pray for an hour or two, it is a whole new dimension. Right now, you are saying, "I don't have that much time." One thing I have learned is people will find the time to do the things that are important to them.

You see the bumper stickers, "Prayer changes things," "Families that pray together stay together," and so on. All of this is true, but do you just want a change, or do you want a supernatural touch from God? Do you want to live a supernatural life? This comes from the quantity of time spent with God. Remember when you met that special someone in your life? You could not spend enough time with him or her. Every waking moment of your life, you thought about that person. You would spend hours together, and then as soon as you arrived at home, you just had to call again.

That's the way we need to be with God. We need to have a burning in our souls to spend time with Him. We need to get serious about our prayer lives.

We need to understand that prayer is the engine that generates supernatural power in our lives.

Ask God to give you a desire to pray and spend time with Him. We can trust God at His Word when He says in Psalm 37:4, *"Delight yourself also in the LORD, And He shall give you the desires of your heart."*

We must also make a commitment to prayer, as it says in His Word: *"Pray without ceasing"* (1 Thess. 5:17). How is this possible? You can't possibly pray twenty-four hours a day, seven days a week, fifty-two weeks a year.

Praying without ceasing is an attitude about prayer.

Whenever something happens in your life, good or bad, do you immediately go to the Lord in prayer? Before you try to handle difficult situations in your everyday routine, do you pray for God to lead you? In your conversations throughout the day, do you pray for God to speak through you? The attitude of *praying first* is what praying without ceasing means. In your anxious moments, times of fear, doubt, or confusion, what do you do?

> *"Be anxious for nothing, but in everything by prayer and supplication, with thanksgiving, let your requests be made known to God"* (Phil. 4:6)

If I ask the question, "Do you believe in God?" most people would answer a resounding, "Yes." Praying without ceasing means that we believe God, not just believe *in* God. We pray with the belief that God will answer. *"Therefore, I say to you, whatever things you ask when you pray, believe that you receive them, and you will have them"* (Mark 11:24).

One of the most powerful prayers we can pray is God's own Word. God loves to hear His words prayed back to Him. Here are some prayers that you can pray from the scriptures back to your Creator.

> *"For God has not given us a spirit of fear, but of power and of love and of a sound mind"* (2 Tim. 1:7).

"God, give me a spirit of power just as You gave the disciples in the book of Acts; enable me to do Your will and truly love my fellow brothers and sisters. Holy Father, continue to help me have a sound mind and take on the mind of Christ."

> And He said to me, "My grace is sufficient for you, for My strength is made perfect in weakness." Therefore most gladly I will rather boast in my infirmities, that the power of Christ may rest upon me. (2 Cor. 12:9)

"Most Heavenly Father, I realize that I am nothing without You. I am a weak vessel and only made strong by Your grace. To win the spiritual battles in my life, I need Your power to help me fight. Help me to continue to realize that I have the power because of who You are in me."

> "And what is the exceeding greatness of His power toward us who believe, according to the working of His mighty power" (Eph. 1:19).

"Thank you, sovereign Lord, for all the spiritual blessings You bestow upon me. It's only by Your supernatural blessings in my life, and the Holy Spirit that lives in me, that I can continue to walk in power in this world and continue winning the battles set before me."

> "Therefore we also pray always for you that our God would count you worthy of this calling, and fulfill all the good pleasure of His goodness and the work of faith with power" (2 Thess. 1:11).

"Thank you, Eternal Father, for making me worthy of Your calling. I am nothing without Your supernatural power to answer Your call on my life and give me the ability to win the spiritual battles I am facing."

> *"Now may the God of hope fill you with all joy and peace in believing, that you may abound in hope by the power of the Holy Spirit"* (Rom. 15:13).

"God of Peace, You give me the joy and peace that I can experience every day through You alone. Please continue to help me walk in Your will so I can have the peace, joy, and hope You give me, by the power of the Holy Spirit."

> *"Behold, I give you the authority to trample on serpents and scorpions, and over all the power of the enemy, and nothing shall by any means hurt you"* (Luke 10:19).

"Mighty Lord, I know I can have victory over temptations. The supernatural power I have through You is much greater than the enemy. I stand victorious because of that supernatural power."

Here are some scriptures you can pray specifically for your life:

In James 4:2, the Bible clearly says, *"You do not have because you do not ask."* When you have a personal relationship with Christ, you can ask Him for the desires of your heart and the gracious God of all the earth provides all your needs. He also gives you what you ask for as long as your heart is right, and it is His will.

Ask of Me, and I will give You the nations for Your inheritance, and the ends of the earth for Your possession. (Ps. 2:8)

⁷Ask, and it will be given to you; seek, and you will find; knock, and it will be opened to you. ⁸For everyone who asks receives, and he who seeks finds, and to him who knocks it will be opened. (Matt. 7:7–8)

If you abide in Me, and My words abide in you, you will ask what you desire, and it shall be done for you. (John 15:7)

Now to Him who is able to do exceedingly abundantly above all that we ask or think, according to the power that works in us. (Eph. 3:20)

¹⁴Now this is the confidence that we have in Him, that if we ask anything according to His will, He hears us. ¹⁵ And if we know that He hears us, whatever we ask, we know that we have the petitions that we have asked of Him. (1 John 5:14–15)

"Gracious God, You tell me that if I only ask, You will give it to me, if it is Your will. Your Word also says I have not because I ask not. Lord, Your Word tells me if I keep on asking, that I will be given what I ask for. If I keep on looking, I will find it. I will see the door open because I keep knocking at the door of prayer.

"Thank You, Father, for allowing me to ask You for anything. It is a privilege for me to pray to the Alpha and Omega, and I never want to take this time spent with You for granted. I also know that if I live for You and make the kingdom of God my primary concern, You will give me all that I need and want from day to day.

"My precious Lord and Savior, I want to walk in power every day of my life. Please give me the boldness to spread Your word and further Your Kingdom.

"God give me the power to take control of all my thoughts and take on the mind of Christ. I want the supernatural ability to overcome all temptations in my life so I can walk in victory.

"Lord, I need wisdom to see the world and lost souls as You see them. I need wisdom to overcome the things of this world that surround me.

"Heavenly Father, help me become totally obedient to your will for my life. I know that this is the only way to peace, joy, and happiness. Lord, help me start to walk in victory today."

The quantity of time spent in prayer determines the power in our lives.

Life is all about ups and downs, twists and turns, mountaintop and valley experiences. God, through His Word, reminds us of this: James 1:2 says, *"My brethren, count it all joy when you fall into various trials."*

As we journey through our spiritual walk and fight the spiritual battles, we must remember, God has a plan for our lives. It does not matter what we have been scarred with because **God never wastes a hurt.**

He wants to use every hurt, disappointment, and abuse to bring honor and glory to Him and help us live a fuller, richer life. I look back on my life, and I was not abused! I was being equipped for the work that God had ahead for me to do.

God is a Life-giving God; He wants us to be life-giving to others. When we are life-giving, we are reflecting the character of Jesus: *"And so it is written, 'The first man Adam became a living being.' The last Adam became a life-giving spirit" (1 Cor. 15:45).*

He wants to give us abundant life, and He wants us to live a life of freedom, walking in victory and winning, as it says in John 10:10: *"The thief does not come except to steal, and to kill, and to destroy. I have come that they may have life, and that they may have it more abundantly."*

God has already secured eternal victory for us. He wants you and me to be victorious in this life and win the spiritual battles.

We don't fight for victory; we fight from a position of victory!

"Call to Me, and I will answer you, and show you great and mighty things, which you do not know" (Jer. 33:3).

No matter what you have been through, are going through or what you're going to go through, God has "great and mighty things" in store you! Our past cannot dictate our future!

We cannot have power in the present and future, holding on to our past.

Go forward and start winning spiritual battles today!

Printed in the USA
CPSIA information can be obtained
at www.ICGtesting.com
LVHW090819221023
761714LV00028B/146